In the Days of Our Undoing

September – November 2020

NATHAN BROWN

MEZCALITA
PRESS

FIRST EDITION, 2021
Copyright © 2021 by Nathan Brown
All Rights Reserved
ISBN-13: 978-1-7348692-3-1

Library of Congress
Control Number: 2021933107

No part of this book may be performed,
recorded, thieved, or otherwise transmitted
without the written consent of the author and
the permission of the publisher. However,
portions of poems may be cited for book
reviews—favorable or otherwise—without
obtaining consent.

Cover Design: Jen Rickard Blair
Back Cover Photograph: Rodney Bursiel

Mezcalita Press, LLC
Norman, Oklahoma

In the Days of Our Undoing

September — November 2020

NATHAN BROWN

About the Pandemic Poems Project:

In The Days of Our Seclusion, [Book 1] is an act of hope in a time when hope has been hard to find. It is an act of community in a time of isolation. It is so much bigger than words on a page. I've had this sneaking feeling that we've never needed poets more than we do right now. Now I know it's true.

~ Beth Wood
Winner of the Oregon Book Awards'
"Readers' Choice" Award
and Kerrville New Folk Award

In the land of the Fire Pit Sessions there's always a glass of something good on the table: a margarita? A cold beer? I pour myself a brew to soften the edges and listen to one of my favorite poets share his words. I envy the fluid lines of Nathan Brown, the unassuming way he goes about dazzling you with insights about a world that seems to have gone crazy. These gorgeous poems—and the beer—are the closest things to a vaccine I've found so far.

~ George Bilgere
Winner of the Pushcart Prize
and May Swenson Poetry Award

Table of Contents

September ... ...
We Had Hoped ... 5
Watertight ... 7
Sorry, But... ... 9
Paws 'n' Claws ... 11
Full of It ... 13
Us, Them, and Others ... 15
Late Summer Weather Report ... 17
A Prayer for My Country ... 19
By a Certain Light ... 21
Lost and Found ... 23
Our Undoing ... 25
Mid Limbo ... 26
Impossibly Simple ... 29
Somewhere in There ... 30
Sacré Bleu ... 32
Covidating ... 34
A Tiny Big Loss ... 36
Dicky Don ... 38
In an Instant ... 39
Red, White, & Seldom Blue ... 41
The Good Doctor ... 42
A Portrait ... 44
I Digress ... 45
Becoming Better Men ... 47
Juncos and Uncles ... 51
My Part ... 53

October ... ...
Beneath It All ... 57
My All ... 59
We Took an Oath ... 62
MGGA ... 64
Let's Hold Our Breath ... 66
Ode to a Good Man Running for Office ... 68
Define Essential ... 70
Happy Someday ... 72
Mostly Mornings ... 74
And I Mean, Everywhere ... 76
It's Not Okay... and That's Okay ... 78
Poet to Poet ... 80
Sourdough I. – The Thing ... 82
Sourdough II. – Endless Rising ... 84
Fly: 1 – Veep: 0 ... 86
For the People ... 88
Un- This, Dis- That, Anti- It All ... 89
Turning Pale ... 91
All in a Day's Voting ... 93
The Full Armor ... 95
I Voted ... 97
Generally Speaking ... 100
Representation ... 102
Reclamation ... 104
Reformation ... 106
Mother of Exiles ... 108
A Fraternal Order of Sorts ... 110
Tandem ... 113

November ... ...
Contingency ... 117
The Biggest Bend Ever ... 118
Better Eons ... 120
The Lights of Marfa ... 121
Chisos Basin ... 123
Roaming a Marathon ... 124
The Longest Day ... 126
Too Much of 'It' ... 127
The Great Delay ... 128
Feet in the Fire ... 130
Who's Who ... 131
Safe and Unsound ... 133
When She Prays ... 135
When He Prays ... 137
When I Pray ... 139
Dot Gov ... 140
Rudy, the Red-Faced ... 142
On Cults and Kool-Aid ... 144
Aftermath ... 146
New Fall Fashion ... 148
Hell Hath No Fury ... 149
Until It's Too Late ... 151
Vast ... 153
The Orangest ... 155
Wet Ingredients ... 157
Let Us Pray ... 158
Black Friday ... 160
Better Than None ... 161

Introduction

In the Days of Our Undoing: September – November 2020, Book 3 of the Pandemic Poems Project, picks up where *In the Days of Our Unrest* leaves off. This book tracks our descent into the political season of the fall, when one of the most significant and perilous elections in our history fomented fear, division, and a deep scarring of this nation. The mental and intellectual devolution of many of our leaders and officials became all too clear, the pandemic surged yet again, with the help of what could be described as an outright materialistic refusal to curb the big block party of consumerism, and we were forced to hold our country up to the mirror for an unprecedented number of reasons—an ongoing abundance of fodder for this daily report.

The Fire Pit Sessions continue to feed the flames of the Pandemic Poems Project. They can be viewed on Nathan's Facebook page:

https://www.facebook.com/chinacoman

If you would like to become a part of this project, in Book 4, contact Nathan or Ashley at mezcalitapress@gmail.com

Acknowledgements

Book 3 is dedicated to those who are struggling, often terribly, with the spiritual, social, and emotional rift that has been caused by diseased politics in this country. Hold on, friends. Stay in the game. We'll get through.

Also to my wife, Ashley. As well as to our friends, Liz McIlravy and Sarah Flournoy, who were the instigators of this endeavor.

Mom, Dad, Sierra… you know by now.

A special thanks to Patrick Marshall, who has been an exceptional supporter of this project, but also, over many years now, a champion of my work and books. I am very grateful, sir.

Finally, I say again, thank you to all those who contributed, both topically and financially, to these books. You have saved a lost year in my career as an artist. Truly. My gratitude springs eternal.

~ Nathan

In the Days of Our Undoing

MEZCALITA
PRESS

September ... ...

We are all born in the middle of the story, and we will all exit before the story is finished.

~ Milton Brasher-Cunningham

We Had Hoped

>   Tuesday, September 1

We had hoped for more
    than this unraveling:

our lives separated out
into like colors, to try
and keep them from
bleeding in the wash;

nationalism as the latest
relapse in the fashion trends
of religion's never-ending catwalk
of torture, martyrdom, and shame;

old, encrusted theology as the hot new
argument for the preservation of racism,
as the most devout among us lay their last
dimes down at the foot of the Antichrist;

Russia, the Cheshire Cat of social media,
playing us all like half-dead mice dangling
from its razor-sharp and radioactive teeth;

capitalism, the ever-widening Continental
Divide, where the rivers now only flow
down to the one sea on the one side;

the novel coronavirus, not so novel
anymore, marching deftly forward,
grazing on ignorance and apathy;

and hope. Yes, we had hoped
for more of that as well…

WATERTIGHT

~ for Jeanne Fell
Wednesday, September 2

Anyone who knows anything
about conspiracy theories
knows that all pizzerias,
like Comet Ping Pong
over in D.C.'s Chevy
Chase neighborhood,
are throbbing hotbeds
for Satanic ritual abuse.

And it's common knowledge
that only Democrats would be
interested in such horror shows.
I mean… where have you been
for the last four, or five, years?

Besides, if *The Washington Post*
thinks their pizza tastes good,
you know Satan is involved.

And of course anyone who
identifies as a '4chan poster'
going by Q Clearance Patriot,
who's ashamed to give a name
because most likely they're not

one person, has to understand
precisely what it is they mean
by "Calm Before the Storm,"
referring to Trump's cryptic
and completely disconnected
from reality account of some
gathering of military leaders
that he apparently managed
to pay attention to for once,
but, all others… including
every intelligence agency
in the world… remain,
somehow, in the dark.

Well… I, for one…
being such the fan
of common sense
that I have always
been, must admit

this one appears
to be about as
watertight as
a frog's ass.

Sorry, But…

> ~ for Gayle Glass
> Friday, September 4

The dog has a right
to feel confused, even
conflicted, about your new
ever-presence around the place.
For so long she believed it was
all she'd ever wanted—for you
to never leave the house again.

But now… there's no time
when she's left in charge.

You're disturbing her
when she is trying
to get her 11 am
beauty rest, there
on your pillow, there
on your bed, that's always
been hers, for these precious
and prescribed hours, most days.

You're getting lazy about the feeding
schedule, and sleeping in… which
pushes back the morning walk,
not to mention other duties.

And, come to think of it,
the two of you haven't been
to the dog park in... what is it
now... weeks... maybe months?

Anyway, what she's trying to say
is... she's afraid this just...
isn't working out.

Paws 'n' Claws

~ for Stoney LeMew
Saturday, September 5

Late in the day,
right around twilight,
soon after we'd carefully
placed the testimonial stones
of our sweet pup's safe-keeping,

we lingered beside the fresh grave,
thoroughly undone by one of life's
terrible inevitabilities… and took
turns weeping and holding each
other in a cloud of incoherence.

In ghostly silence, our impish
tan-gray and white rescue cat,
Stoney, appeared from the dim
shadows of the fire pit's walls
and let out a low moan-cry.

His belovéd older sister…
of a long-nosed species…
had helped him adjust to
his new life and territory
with an immense patience.

In our old girl's very last days,
when she couldn't see or hear,
he would come up to lean into
and rub against her neck, then
wrap his tail around her nose.

And whatever I may have ever
believed about those made of fur
and paws—or hooves, or feathers
and claws—was completely altered,
once again, in our next holy moment.

He laid the entire length of his body
in the dirt by her stones... moaned
again... then placed his two front
paws on the rock near his face...
not moving for a minor eternity.

I don't know what I mean to say,
but that's never stopped me. So...
something's telling me that there is
something these highly sentient souls
are trying to tell us... that could save
our grandchildren from extinction.

Full of It

~ Pam Gunsten
Sunday, September 6

A cocktail glass
was designed for two
ounces of liquor, an ounce
of tonic or juice… and maybe,
a little liqueur… or a few olives…
that's why you don't make a margarita
in a beer mug. Lives would be lost.
A beer mug was built for more,
as well as much bigger guts.

Capitalism's glass
doesn't believe
in bottoms…
or measuring
the ingredients.
No, it's going for
a never-ending pour.
The problem is, physics.

And yet, Americans are hard-
liners when we get to drinking…
so it's gonna take a mighty bouncer
to kick us out of this bacchanalian bar.

That said, the mighty bouncer cometh,
in a storm of wind and fire, riding on
the nimbostratus of a hurricane—
a fine drink as well, by the way.

And so we best redesign
our glass, before that
mighty hand lands
on our sotted
shoulders,
and says,

> *enough*
> *already.*

US, THEM, AND OTHERS

> ~ for Candace Mary Osterhout
> Tuesday, September 8

Some of us forget
that, for others, the job
does not come back, and so,
for many of those, the lease does
run out, which leaves most of these
with no options to speak of…
except for the few of them
who have parents they
can move back in with.

For some, it's fortunate.
For others, not so much.
But… for all… the stresses
are numerous and mounting.

Job hunting during a pandemic?
It's plenty hell enough without one.

Does the love of parents have limits?
Depends… but their patience does.

So, wherever we are… all of us…
all of them… we sit and listen to
the news of a government that

loves to pretend it cares about all
of them, and us. But the streets
are packed with thousands of
those who do not trust it…

nor the police—some
good, but others bad—
who are mostly wanting
to keep the job they have.

Which leaves most of us, them,
and the others too, with no idea
who, in this world, we *can* trust.

Which leaves the lucky among us,
who have at least one someone
we do trust… realizing just
how lucky we really are.

Late Summer Weather Report

~ for all those in the path
Wednesday, September 9

Seven and a half hours
of rain on a windshield
is a few too many for me,
the wipers keeping no time
to any sad song I could find.

And all in a land that should
be in Stage 4 drought status
in its own little burning hell,
not dipping down below 60°
in the early part of September.

They're shoveling snow, I hear,
up in Denver. But my one friend
out in Anaheim tells me the sky
is a gray-orange, and he's got
a thick layer of ash covering
the surface of his new pool.

There may be very little left
of California… after the dry
lightning and Santa Ana winds
have said what they have to say.

Meanwhile, from Corpus Christi
to Connecticut, folks I care about
are keeping eyes peeled on Paulette
and Rene, as their anger takes shape
somewhere in the warming Atlantic.

A Prayer for My Country

> Thursday, September 10

Having traveled almost every state
in this reeling nation—still trying
to make it to Maine if you know
someone there who might help
a poet out—I know what it is
I want to save from the way
Republicans tend to think…

ownership and automated gates,
private schools… for our own,
opportunity for advancement,
for those implicitly ordained.

What I don't know, is how
a violent, viral shaking, down
to our core, will affect the way
we see each other when it's over.

If our era unlocks its jaw, we will all
have to readjust to the light when
we fall out of that dark mouth.

Our pupils will dial back…
and we will pause, before
we make some choices.

Will we question unchecked consumption…
for the way that it defies the laws of physics?

Or, just bow heads back down to phones?

Will we run the math that when more
and more goes to those who have
the most to begin with, they will
become fewer and fewer, which
leaves less and less for those with
little to begin with, so their numbers
become more and more—an equation
that needs no historical margin of error?

Or, just watch the finale of the Kardashians
one more time, because we miss it, so much?

Will we realize the Great American Road
is bound by those mighty parenthetical
brackets of the Pacific and Atlantic,
and that we can never travel on it
for the first time, ever again?

Or not?

BY A CERTAIN LIGHT

~ for Audrey Streetman
Friday, September 11

Thank God the Chinese
figured out how to make
candles out of whale fat
before the Dark Ages...

before Jesus even, come
to give John his reason
to write a first chapter
where a "light shines
in the darkness..."

as well as the Knights
of the Round Table their
reason to fervently search
for the lovely and elusive
idea of the Holy Grail.

By the 13th century,
candle-making had
become an industry,
a "guild craft" it was
called, by the English
and the French. Only,
the French had a much

prettier word for it…
like their word for candle,

    chandelle   (geez…)

But we don't need candles now.
We have electricity and glass
bulbs for our light. And…
when power goes out…
we have AA batteries
and incandescent lamps.

But in this current darkness,
the only thing my mom wants
to pray by, out in her cave
of an art studio,
is candles…

their light
is just different.

And even God agrees.

Lost and Found

~ Karen Zundel
Saturday, September 12

Do we lose ourselves
in a good book? Or,
do we find ourselves
somewhere in there?

My guess would be
it's whichever one
we need the most
in a given moment.

Or, maybe it's just
one long, lascivious
game of hide 'n' seek
we play with ourselves.

Either way, here in this
terminally slow season,
when we have all been
asked to occupy most

of our hours in a day
with ourselves, few
are better prepared
than the librarians.

They chose superior
friends much earlier
in life and, therefore,
are now well-equipped.

There is no isolation…
when one is surrounded
by a swarm of archetypes
engulfed in turbulent plots.

And there is no cabin fever
when, all through breakfast,
we're traipsing among yellow
daffodils in the Lake District,

and then, half way into lunch,
we find ourselves adrift… and
a little frightened… somewhere
in the teeming alleys of Calcutta.

Next thing we know, we've landed
on an unknown planet, with hopes
to settle it… because, at this point?
that… is what we are all dying for.

OUR UNDOING

> ~ for Betty Potts
> Sunday, September 13

Before it means
our ruination, or
downfall, undoing
can also be… say…
an opening, loosening,
or unfastening of a thing.

Those three actions seem to say,
"Here's what you could do, before
your destruction, to try and mitigate
the ridiculous mess you've created."

In other words… the dictionary is
trying to give us a possible way out.

Mid Limbo

> ~ for Anne Harris
> Tuesday, September 15

There's that last person
to leave the big party…
who just has one more
story they want to tell,
then, and they swear,
they will let you go.

There's a two-time
survivor… waiting
for the next round
of her test results.

Or the soldier…
who is entangled,
impaled, and stuck
in the barbed wire,
bombs and bullets
hailing all around,
but none to bring
a peace he needs,
the rest that he
would die
to have.

It's when
the liminal
becomes
eternal.

A change
is gonna come.

But no one thought
it would require years,
let alone a few hundred?

There will be no vaccine for
willful ignorance, the abuses
of office and power, nor for
ten generations of racism...

There's no cure for the bald
and bearded dumbass who
rips off another's mask
and spits in her face...

There is no user's guide
for rewiring the sad brain
of a Gen Z-er who would
kill his own grandmother
for an all-night kegger...

It's hard to breathe
all that hot, filthy air.

And yet, here we stand,
amid the smoke, the wind,
and these charred remains,

wondering who among us
will be the one to pick up
the smoldering flag…

and march onward.

IMPOSSIBLY SIMPLE

~ for Anne Harris
Wednesday, September 16

The next hardest thing
humans will ever do

is escape the virtual
existence of screens,

switch them all off,
open front doors,

and step out, into
that great increase

of a sun's radiance,
as well as radiation,

then stand in stunned
silence at that docket

of a thousand crimes,
before kneeling to tend,

with soft and weak hands,
the wounds of the Earth.

SOMEWHERE IN THERE

~ for Anne Harris
Thursday, September 17

If we let the quiet in,
give it time to roam
our neural hallways,
filled with the chatter
between the frontal lobe
and the amygdala—where
emotions used to live,
                       instead
of switching on Wolf Blitzer's
The Situation Room on CNN…

If we let all of this alone time
simmer in a pot of quarantine
over the low heat of candles,
maybe with some hot tea,
or a little rosé,
                       instead
of bouncing back and
forth between Twitter
and Facebook and…

If we let the longer
hours of this life-
as-unusual chew

on the gristly bone of our
relentless discontent
and dread,
          instead
of binging
on Candy Crush,
Angry Birds Evolution,
or Words with Friends,

the liminal may be able
to cook up its mystical
and mercurial alchemy.

We may choose better
friends, and enemies,
when all this is over.

We may even find
what is really
going on
below.

Sacré Bleu

~ John Hoag
Friday, September 18

As familiarity reaches
the point that it breeds
underwear draped over
the edge of the bathtub,

that's when we begin to
realize it will take more
than hormones to keep
the thing, the love, alive.

Dealbreakers tend to be
unambiguous. The issue
either is, or isn't, one…

like strangely large feet;
which way, over or under,
the toilet paper should roll
out of the holder on the wall;
or the level at which the trash
beneath the kitchen sink should
be considered full enough to go.

The sense of smell determines,
more than any other, the limits

of love. And that's why, when
he gathered that she thought
the Camembert, or Fourme
d'Ambert, or, mon Dieu…
that Raclette from the Alps,
smelled just like dirty socks,
he wasn't sure it could work.

Not when it comes to cheese.

Covidating

> ~ for Jody Karr
> Saturday, September 19

So, stinky cheese?
Red, white, or no
wine? Boxers, or
briefs? Questions
that need answers…
before this thing goes
any further. Some can be
talked out? But Zoom will
not reveal how bad the breath
smells… or one's taste in shoes.

At least that looming issue of sex
on the first date is less complicated
on Facetime, than at the front door.

It seems we're talking more now,
in these weird days, which…
might, or might not, be
a positive thing?

But then the problem
of lighting. How we look
on camera. And, that poster
we forgot on the wall behind us.

Chemistry, when bodies
don't come together…
will need new science.

But this way, we won't
have to fight over who
is going to pay the tab.

Wait, is that country
music we hear,
in the room
next door?

Anyway…

it's nice to meet us.

A Tiny Big Loss

> ~ for Ruth Bader Ginsberg
> Sunday, September 20

I know of five
complete bastards
in Washington D. C.
who were happy to see
you go. But, you were in
the business. So, they will
come as no surprise to you.

For 27 years, your graceful
yet slightly wicked wink
and a nod told us all
we needed to know.

And in those years,
you faithfully delivered
the goods—for the good,
the bad, and the outright evil
alike—as you saw to be right.

It's not a secret I wanted you
for our President. The thugs,
politicians every one, simply
are not working out for us.

We needed a Mother Mary
meets Mata Hari, a Thelma
or Louise come St. Teresa,

a petite, atomic bomb of…
decency and determination.

Dicky Don

> ~ for Dave Charlson
> Monday, September 21

The dickiest of dicks was Don,
and the tiniest johnny was John's.
That's why all the Dons 'n' Johns
are always the loudest ones…

at parties they throw for Janes,
with yacht and penthouse brains,
who marry the Dons for the planes,
the Johns despite their varicose veins.

It is the saddest of the sad old scenes…
these Dons, and Janes, Jills 'n' Jeannes…
Gucci suits, boob jobs, burned out dreams,
and ten-thousand-dollar ripped blue jeans.

But, the dickiest of all the dicky Dons,
and the lesser-endowed johnny Johns,
would have to be the one of all ones,
who goes by both Donald and John.

In an Instant

> ~ for Persephone,
> goddess of the autumnal equinox
> Tuesday, September 22

On the spring equinox
I wrote of the clearing
skies in Shanghai, and
the dolphins returning
to the canals of Venice.

It was the second poem
in what's now turned out
to be the Pandemic Poems
Project. At that time, though,
I'd simply thought I was writing
the morning's piece in my journal.

The autumnal equinox, possibly
my favorite salutation in every
year, occurred some twenty
and three minutes ago.

It symbolizes a release
from the torture chamber
of August, the crematorium
that never, quite, ashes you.

We experience equal parts
light and darkness—which
brings back a spiritual keel
that feels a bit truer to life,
the best we can hope for…

like sitting on a front porch
in Texas with cloud cover,
damp ground, and 68°—
a thing I would've thought
impossible just a week ago.

And even though I'm happy
I didn't know, six months ago,
what I still don't understand…

I think I'll sit a while and revel
in this unlikely scenario, this
excruciatingly rare instant,
of absolute equality…

that only happens
two times a year.
At least here…
on this planet.

Red, White, & Seldom Blue

~ for Linda Basinger
Wednesday, September 23

I tread lightly in the deep-red
states of my birth and raising.
I come from the loins of good
old kin who vote to keep them
that crimson shade of blood—
because… they shed a lot of it
to survive in these territories.

And whatever color you want
to believe flows in my veins,
those same people, in their
never-ending seasons of
planting, harvesting and
quoting scriptures, also
showed me the ultimate
consequences of a God
sticking a blood-stained,
8-foot tall, 10-foot wide,
political sign on the barb-
wire fence of heaven's hard-
earned, boundless acreage…
and just who and how many,
will never be welcome there.

The Good Doctor

~ for Dr. Anthony Fauci
Thursday, September 24

Your confusion over why people
wouldn't want to just be good,
considerate of others… was
oddly, almost childishly,
genuine.
         Your sense
of bafflement over
the joyful ignorance
of pot-bellied Bubbas
in their desperate need to
have their boats and bikinis,
wine coolers and beer brauts,
and, eat them too, out there
on the Lake of the Ozarks,
made you pull at your tie,
put your head in your hands.

That's why, when your patience,
which has been monolithic and
long-suffering, finally ran out
with Senator Rand Paul, likely
because of a ridiculous hairdo
as much as his relative idiocy,

I felt comforted, relieved a bit,
at the sight of your resolute eyes
and pointed finger sitting him back
down on his posh congressional ass.

And I thought, O Doctor! my Doctor!

Yes, good doctor, more of that please.

A Portrait

> ~ for Vice President Mike Pence
> Friday, September 25

You have the eyes
of a dormant volcano...
the brow of a dark mountain
shredded back in the Precambrian.

The steam and magma that once
fired your faith in an angry,
vengeful God has since
hardened into razor-
sharp pumice lying
in the high desert
of a stony face.

A jaw... so set...
teeth... petrified...
the remains in a Valley
of Dry Bones that Ezekiel
himself wouldn't dare cross.

Lips so thin, and ossified,
only the Four Horsemen
of the Apocalypse could
break them into a smile.

I Digress

> ~ for Eric Clow
> Saturday, September 26

What if turning around
did not signal a defeat?

What if homecoming
was not a regression?

What if backwards
were the only means
for us to go forwards?

What if the theology
of capitalism is flawed,
and it turns out that less
is the only land that will
take us in when the bell
on Wall Street tolls for
tumbleweeds and turtle
doves, instead of some
flock of blue silk suits?

What if that day arrives,
when all the tired clichés
come home… you know,
to roost… and we find out

that it was… in fact…
a small world… and
that those people
in glass houses
finally threw
one too many
stones.
        And yet…
the extra mile wasn't
all that far… nor was
square one all that bad
when we got back to it.

So, why would it surprise
anyone that letting go is…

the only way we're ever
going to hold on
to whatever
is left.

Becoming Better Men

~ Robert Dean Kennedy, Uncle Bob
Sunday, September 27

"A man of complete integrity.
If one ever lived, it was Bob
Kennedy." When a younger,
and an only, sister can say that
about a man? we know we are
dealing with truly rarefied air…
especially if she also uses a word
like "ornery," when she divulges
his love to tease her, and others.

When a man rode the early half
of the twentieth century through
the Navy Air Corps on the wings
of his saxophone, into ownership
of a large furniture manufacturing
company, and, eventually, Mayor
of Belton, Texas—he even has
a street named for him there—

and when his word, once given,
was an absolute bond, much like
a friend, once made, is a brother
or sister for life, we note a fine
portrait of a man who spent life

in service to what that century
was trying to make better in men.

And, when he came home to visit,
on leave from the Corps in the 40s,
you could bet that he knew where
Kilroy was, and that he'd paint it
in big black letters on a beautiful
white gate his father had built out
in their backyard on 41st in Tulsa.

And, when he'd take off running
in the hall of his boarding house
at UT Austin to slide across the
baby grand in the parlor—much
to the horror of the landlady—
you could be sure he'd scored
fairly well on his I.Q. test.

And, if you noticed my shift
in verb tense in these stanzas?
it's because at some point during
the writing of this poem, they will
have made the decision to turn off
the machines and remove the tubes,

                and... release him.

I have one uncle on each side of the family-
tree branch above. And this, my mother's
brother, will be my first one to lose…
a decent man… one who represents
the most critical qualities we will need
to see in more men, to survive this age.

He was, one cousin might say, an overly
strict father. But one whose love always,
eventually, overcame fear or disapproval.

He was unwavering, a lifelong conservative
who, towards the end, was able to concede
that a Republican president had gone bad.

He loved animals, good wine, children.
But especially birds. He loved to bake
bread, supply the BBQ for gatherings.

And trees. Even his 'artsy' nephew,
the poet, he'd welcome to his home,
to share a glass of the good, despite
knowing quite well where that artsy
nephew stood—at least I suspect—
on what was driving the nation down,

because… he adored the nephew's
mom, his little sister, for 87 years,

even if his kid sister has to leave
a room if Trump's face appears
on the TV screen.
                      He *loved* her,
until his death, at 93, undid
the earthly aspects of it.

A simple thing,
that could un-do
much of the wrong
we've gone and done,
in the name of heaven,
all over a wounded world.

Juncos and Uncles

> Monday, September 28

It was a small thing.
A Dark-eyed Junco.
We had just settled in
to a ridiculously scenic
cabin, outside of Pagosa
Springs. Ashley had barely
warmed her wood deckchair
on the back porch, with a hot
cup of coffee, and a crazy view
of the San Juan Mountain Range,
when this tiny gray ball of feathers
smashed into a large picture window
over her left shoulder. It fell, belly up,
on a slat of the brown deck by her feet.

After a small scream, she welled up…
with those tears of "What do I do?"

I jumped up and ran over to them.
"They sometimes come out of it,
right?" she near pleaded.
                      I softly
stuttered… because sometimes
they do, but I didn't like the look
of this one's odds.

She stayed with it
anyway… because animals are too
much for her. Especially the small,
cute, and fluffy varieties. And so,
when I knelt down to look into
a glossy dark eye, for a sign,
it mentioned it was time…

time to check in with mom
about Uncle Bob.
                    Her text
back to me read:

   He left us about 5:30

I looked at the clock: 5:39.

I stepped over to kneel, again,
by the dark eyes. They had lost
some of the shine, were slowly
closing, from the gentle stroke
of Ashley's finger filled with
a last bit of ferocious hope.

I went to look for a shovel.

My Part

> Wednesday, September 30

It is 81°… at 4:22 pm…
here in Pagosa Springs, Colorado
on Wednesday, September 30, 2020.

My bare toes are soaking up a coolish
alpine breeze somewhere a little left
of the heart of the United States.

The average electric bill in this
increasingly average country is
$117.65 a month. The average

lifespan is 78.9 years… that's
in the neighborhood of 947.999
months, so at an average life's end,

that average life has spent an average
of right at $111,532.082 on electricity…
according to a poet's suspect calculations.

I think about numbers and stuff like this.
It's why I'm not a therapist, or a forest
ranger, or social worker. Something

useful. It is also why I glance at
every light switch that I walk by…
unplug every hotel room television.

And it's why I've learned to navigate
every inch of my house in darkness.
And it's why I love the moon, put in

two extra super-reflecting skylights,
eat leftover pizza or pea soup cold.
All of which, when it comes to my

daughter's future, is…
I suppose…
useful?

October ... ...

for what was Christ if not God's desire
to smell his own armpit?

~ Chris Abani
The New Religion

Beneath It All

> ~ for Catherine Lanham
> Thursday, October 1

The young girl walking home after class
asked the wise old man, pushing an empty
shopping cart down the sidewalk on Main,

Who will hold up my best friend who had to leave school early today, because she is very sick, if I'm not there to do it?

Her mom will do it, the old man assured.

But who'll hold up her mom if she catches it too?

Her father, he replied.

But who will hold up both of them when an ambulance takes them to a hospital because they're much sicker than my friend?

There will be a nurse who will take special care of both her parents.

But what about when it gets worse and they have to go into the ICU?

A good doctor will do his very best.

But who will hold up my friend if they don't come out? And who will hold up the doctor, the nurse, and the ambulance driver, when it all just happens too many times?

There will be relatives, counselors, ministers, and a team of psychologists.

But who'll hold up all of them when there's finally too much crying and dying and crying?

The old man scratched, and then tugged at, his ragged beard, and considered his next move thoughtfully, before making it.

The poet.

The girl looked, first at the empty cart, then up at him suspiciously, knowing she had him now. *And what holds up the poet?*

Oh, honey, he smiled,
  his gray eyes glinting…
    it's poets all the way down.

My All

> ~ for all my fellow, hardworking artist friends
> Friday, October 2

Without posting a sexy picture
or a cute GIF to go with it,
Mark asks a question
on social media,
in big letters:

> **Where are the voices of
> musicians, writers, and
> artists to lead us out
> of this mess?**

He went on to lament
about how we were so
much better in the 1960s.

Well, Mark, I can only speak
for me. I have been on the job
for 40 years. The mess is a lot
older than you seem to think.

I have written a poem every
day for over 20 years now.
I've been writing songs
since I was thirteen.

Some of the earlier ones
weren't too exceptional.
But, my recent album?
I'm quite proud of it.
It has a song, "Rise,"
that might interest you.
You should also check out
my version of "Get Together"
by The Youngbloods, in the 58th
episode of The Fire Pit Sessions
that I've been live streaming
for a number of months.

I have driven some three
to five hundred thousand
miles (math is not my gift;
drives the tax lady crazy…)
with books and CDs stuffed
into a suitcase or a car trunk,
with a guitar in the back seat,
or stuck in the overhead bin.

I played one time for a crowd
of three at a house concert…
another time, at Sultan's Pool,
just outside the ancient walls
of the Old City of Jerusalem,

for an audience of 10,000,
who were all waving lighters
by the close of the final song.

I survived about twelve years
without any health insurance.
And, the policy I have now?
It would be cheaper to die.

I will receive nothing… no
thing in the way of benefits
from the retirement package
I never had enough to start.

This poem will appear in my
24th book.
         And I'm not sure
what more you're wanting of
us—the musicians, writers,
and artists—but this one
struggles every day with,
and for, the cause, strives
to help out a limping world,
busts his ass…   and, now…
asks… "What are you doing?"

We Took an Oath

> ~ for Dr. Sean Conley
> Saturday, October 3

I considered avoiding the topic.
I hope that will at least help…
a little… when you wish I had?

But when it comes to the un-pre-
meditated mission of the Pandemic
Poems, I have taken a devilish oath.

After driving one of the Southwest's
highways that causes a soul to burn
anew with desire for this country,

we pulled into Loma Encantada,
above Santa Fe, and I committed
an act of opening up Facebook—

Pandora's newest software version
of her notorious box—to discover
President Trump finally had Covid.

The great denier come down with
the virus of his denial. However,
fear not, all my fellow patriots,

as well as less-regarded citizens,
for Walter Reed shall supply him
the finest health and medical care

known to science. And the good
Walter shall supply it despite his
relentless efforts to deny it, and

everything it has ever stood for,
because medical science requires
a solemn oath, named for an old

Greek physician that the President
would be loath to try to pronounce.
"Hip… Hippo… Hippawhatever."

So, I am now imagining a classic
Greek tragedy that is playing out
in the doctor's mind, as he treats

this fountain of furious ignorance,
who discounts for a world to hear,
the very discipline he has devoted

his life to… the very discipline
that will be forced to preserve
the purveyor of its destruction.

MGGA

> Sunday, October 4

If he lives,
he will be the new
Messiah to his minions…
all hoping just to touch a hem
of his insanely big black overcoat,
believing it will heal them of diversity.

He'll be the last coming of Christ…
so great, we'll never need another,
with the power to turn water into
the vinegar of eternal vindication.

With the Supreme Court sealed up,
he will take his rightful place among
the Holy Trinity, the Son-come-lately.
I mean, who needs Jesus anyway?
Hippies are losers… all Peace,
Love, and Whatever the Hell.

Let's Make God Great Again.
Reclaim him in the angry name
of the Old Testament. The God
we could rely on to drown legions
of brown people with black beards
in thunderous waves of the Red Sea,

to rain fire down from the heavens
on those who don't attend church
three times a week, and to accept
daughters as burned sacrifices…

just like the one old Jephthah
offered up to him… back
in the Book of Judges.

Let's Hold Our Breath

> Monday, October 5

He could be ravaged
by epiphany, struck by
a secret service flashlight
on the road to Damascus.

Stigmata could, suddenly,
appear on his little hands,
wrists, and feet, shocking
him to see that he bleeds.

If the drug cocktails, there
at Walter Reed, hit just right,
an image of the Virgin Mary
might appear in burnt toast.

And once he realizes she has
come on divine business, not
to lose her virginity, he may,
finally, shut up and listen…

sprouting a tumor of empathy
on his barbed and crippled soul,
one the doctors will refuse to cut
out, to save millions of other lives.

He may even beg forgiveness
for having crucified his own
medical and scientific saviors.
There's a history of impossibility.

Yes… he could rise, using the shiny
rails of his privileged hospital bed,
changed, now bent on reversing
every decision he's ever made.

ODE TO A GOOD MAN
  RUNNING FOR OFFICE

~ for Bryce Barfield
Tuesday, October 6

The first thing they will go for
is a knee sweep, to take your
legs out from under you,
or even break them.

You stand for 10,000
years of the slight chance
that they might lose power.

Then comes the anger. Not just
that of the idiots on the other side
with nothing else, or left, to do…
but yours, at the insanities they
will claim in your good name.

Another thing, find out early
where their money hides…
meaning, up which asses.
Those are the asses with
more time, resources,
and video footage of
you saying what you
really feel about them.

Whatever cocktail parties
they choose to show up at?
Leave... as soon as possible.

Anything you say can and will be
a lie to the opposition. Everything
you do will be misrepresented,
misconstrued, misreported,
and every other miss there is.

And I had wanted to help you.
It may not seem that's the case.
But, I had to make all this clear
before swinging the ship around.

If no one with a 5th-grade education
believes any thing a politician says...
or does... then... your only chance
is to 'be' someone that the others
can't quite wrap their besotted,
one-track, and befuddled
brains around.

                    Candidate for Oklahoma House of
          Representatives District 26 in Shawnee, OK

Define Essential

> ~ for Bonnie Eissler
> Wednesday, October 7

The government has long
considered poets to be
nonessential workers.

So, we were out of a job
well before the lockdown
sent all of the others home.

And we would like to offer
our condolences. It's never
felt good to be unnecessary.

And yet, I know of essentials
who would've given anything
to be catalogued as otherwise.

As the months wear on, though,
we've begun to redefine the two.
Turns out, it's not all that simple.

Up in Denver they briefly deemed
liquor store employees to be nons.
But, when the entire city panicked,

went mile high, people forming lines
a mile or so long, store owners toting
loaded pistols, they quickly rescinded.

But now, as we reassess government,
an increasing number of Americans
appear to be thinking that the most

non-essential worker of them all
might just be the one squatting
up there in the highest office.

Happy Someday

> ~ for Christa Pandey
> Thursday, October 8

Every latest design feature
of the smartphone's camera
gets better at hiding the way
we look to a person who is
actually standing before us.

We fondle all the apples
in the bin until we find one
worthy of sacrificing to a god.
The one that doesn't remind us
of our own blemishes and bruises.

We drive around, up and down,
to find a parking space closer
to the front doors of a big-
box megastore, because
it saves us something.
Like, time… right?

We believe the drug
with the pretty name
and its 37 side effects
will make us as happy
as the lady raising her

smiling child up toward the sun
in a commercial with the grave
voice going off like an AK-47
in the last 20 muted seconds.

And, why don't farmers stop
using DDT and Glyphosate,
while still delivering unto us
plump, buxom cantaloupes
and watermelons that glisten
in the mist of a produce aisle
with pornographic perfection?

Just one more shot of Botox
should make that SOB sorry
he ever laid eyes on that girl.

Besides, there's no huge slice
of rose-petaled wedding cake
we can't have, and eat as well,
that Spanx can't help cover up.

And what good is the purse, or
a closet, with an empty pocket,
or an unused shelf, left inside?

Mostly Mornings

> ~ for me
> Friday, October 9

Dark nimbus clouds
have a steel-trap hold
on the sky this morning,
but I don't think that's it.

My Kashi protein waffle
and low-acid coffee are
now cold, for how long
I have sat here, staring
at the page with nothin',
not a damn thing, to say.

Not often, in more than
twenty years of mornings,
has that happened to me.

However, for the last 205
of these mostly mornings,
maybe the rare afternoon,
I have, mostly, considered
the fears and joys, hopes,
yet disbeliefs, occasional
gains, and major losses,
of… mostly… others,

            from the lack
of toilet paper on shelves,
to severe, urban loneliness.
From new romance tucked in
to the glow of welcome isolation,
to the death of a beloved spouse—
by way of what the year's been about.

So… one of the poetry commissioners
of this thoroughly unplanned adventure
had warned me of a tollbooth up ahead.
And I was not stupid enough to ignore
one as wise as this one's proven to be.

But… I carry this torch… one that
often burns my face. And I've paid
long and dearly to earn the license.
I'm just asking… of one of you…
who listens in… who still reads…
who understands this mission…
could you hold it for me? Only
for a night… so I can sit here,
by this fire for a while, maybe
lean my head back to look up
at the stars, while I remind
myself… why I do this.

AND I MEAN, EVERYWHERE

> ~ for Karen Zundel
> Saturday, October 10

Signs, signs, everywhere a sign…

And the Five Man Electric Band
had no idea how bad the signs
would get… some fifty years
down the road. Especially
roads like Highway 281
among the Texas hills
where every pipe-rail
gate has an 8x12-foot
piece of **TRUMP 2020**
zip-tied to rusty joints.

Or, just about any road
between, say, Allentown
and Pittsburgh way down
in the southern half, so red,
Pennsylvania's eyes bleed—

where, if you wanna play Jesus
about politics, they'd be thrilled
to make you a crown of barbwire.

Signs, signs, everywhere a sign…

once one of God's most useful
tools in his big divine box...

and now, not even he
can get a word in
edgewise.

It's Not Okay… and That's Okay

~ for Bonnie Eissler
Sunday, October 11

We don't need to number our griefs.
I recall one friend, I no longer see,
who held down a second job as
a remind-er that she had more
griefs than me… the remind-ee.

We need not measure them either.
There are those in every gathering
whose griefs began at their birth.
And psychologists now speak of
an ancestral grief. A grief so long,
we don't speak of it in mere years.

Then comes the question of depth.
Back in my Ultimate Frisbee phase,
a time of blood, sweat, and cleats,
I remember this one older player,
the Dude, who we eventually lost
to the Mariana Trench of Grief.
He swam down so far, into that
oceanic embrace, with its intense
marine pressure, his sorry lungs
couldn't have survived a return

to the surface any more than
they did staying down there.

And what of collective grief,
the grief of an entire species?
Even though few are talking
about it, most of the others
fathom what it is that they
are not ready to talk about.

Which brings us to the idea
of ambiguous loss, a No-Step
Program with no clear and easy
suggestions to guide us through
to anything resembling closure.

      My griefs are mine.
          Yours are yours.
Hers will forever be numbered.
His took him all the way under.

So, let us bake cookies, and leave
them in tins on each other's porch.
No platitudes attached… Thanks.
And let us write poems that say:
  I hear you… and… it is true.
  And…   yes…   it hurts.

POET TO POET

~ for Bonnie Lynn, in memory of Bob Lynn
Monday, October 12

We knew what was not
in it for us… all along.
Those who'd wanted
something from it…
learned to play guitar.

An undergrad with a pen,
a leather journal, a backpack,
and a new fire-red Mustang GT
that dad just bought him, who's got
the whole summer ahead of him
with no plans for a job…
    is not a poet…
no matter how many
coffeehouses he haunts…
in no matter how many towns
he pulls into on so many highways.

The real poet is the one who sulks
and exasperates his family when
he can't carve out enough time
to scribble some metaphor
singing, like an earworm,
in an ever-distracted mind.

The poet is legion—that mad
man in a cemetery with enough
voices in his head to drive a herd
of pigs off a cliff edge into the sea,

the one who finally settled down a bit
when Jesus took the time to listen…
and appeared to understand him.

If the majority speaks and reads
in sentences and paragraphs…

the business of lines and stanzas
can become a pretty lonely one…

but, when you've been over there,
and seen the mindbending beauty
of that weird and wondermous
alternate universe of words,
what's a poor soul to do?

Sourdough I. – The Thing

> ~ for Beth Lavinder
> Tuesday, October 13

7,000 years and, let's say,
for the fun of it, 209 days
ago, someone mixed equal
parts flour and water, and
then had to leave it sitting
on the counter… because,
let's say, the damned kids
were fighting again, so…
one of them went crying
off into the woods, again,
and hasn't been seen now
for several hours or more.

Having forgotten about it,
for all of the family strife,
someone came in to find
the next morning, that
their little mixture of
flour and water had
more than tripled
in size overnight.

Apparently…
the thing had,

let's say, gorged
itself, on itself, and
gained a lot of weight.

Science had not devised
the term 'fermentation' yet.
So… someone had to describe
what happened some sort of way.

Anyway, the oven's been smoldering
for some 24 hours now, and all these
grumbly kids need something to eat.

So, in goes the big fat dough baby
and – voilà – a new bread is born.

Though French didn't exist yet.
Which is why I could not call
the thing *levain*. But, those
French eventually came
along. And so, that
is what we call it,
the thing, now.

Sourdough II. – Endless Rising

~ for Beth Lavinder
Wednesday, October 14

Flour… water… and salt.
   Hydration, fermentation.
      Baker's percentage.

As a poem, sourdough
proves itself a haiku.

    Time…
   temperature,
  slap and fold…

As a science, sourdough
relates to the tectonic plates,
and the formation of continents.

Autolysis…
   an odd act of
      self-digestion.

As a mythology, sourdough
dances on the edges of art.
Destruction as the means
of regeneration, creation,
the Phoenix of all breads.

The patient kneading,
a need of measured waiting,
the arduous and acidic muscling,
the hard, long working of it,
decades of endless rising.

As a philosophy, sourdough
smells like a fresh new loaf
of what we've almost lost
in the pandemonium
of progress.

Fly: 1 – Veep: 0

> ~ for Tina Crittendon Baker
> Thursday, October 15

Musca domestica, a dipteran insect
which lays its eggs in excrement
and decaying organic matter
and spreads disease…

Love how the Oxford
dictionary calls a spade
a "common housefly."

And look, I've had one
land on me, but I don't
recall allowing it to stay
long enough to lay some
75 to 150 eggs in my hair.

Then again, I don't tend
to wear a helmet when
I perform on a stage.
My hair's thinning.
I would sense it.

And the idea of a fly
going viral is delightful
as *double entendre* goes, no?

But, you can bet it's a rock star,
now, among all its fellow flies,
who always seem to be glued
to some television screen.

If a debate were a rodeo,
man, that thing hung on
to all that bull for a good
chunk of a brief lifetime.

Was it a protest? For all
hexapod invertebrates?
Who are likely as upset
about this administration's
lax stance on climate change?

Or, was he just playing clown
in the Traveling Flea Circus?

Either way, few could miss
the multiple metaphors
at work, and play,
in the moment.

For the People

> ~ for Senate Majority Leader McConnell
> Friday, October 16

Dear Mitch,
there comes a point
in the life of every senator
when the world is simply moving
too much faster, all around and past,
than your wide eyes and cadaver neck
can register anymore. You look to be
more baffled than anything else—
there are headlights everywhere…
and you seem ever caught in them.

Though reluctant… Michael Jordan
knew when it was finally time to put
the basketball down, and walk away.
Though I am not suggesting that you
do underwear commercials for Hanes.

But, it might be time for the quiet life,
somewhere in the hills outside of town.

And, if not for yourself… then…
please… do it for the world.

Un- This, Dis- That, Anti- It All

~ for the undecided voter
Saturday, October 17

I too am undecided,
even though I know
who I am voting for.

Because I too remain
unconvinced there are
any bodies serving us?

And maybe we're undone
by this congressional house,
in which both of the chambers
are crawling with creepy hoarders
who can barely squeeze down aisles
between piles and piles of rotting shit.

And, maybe we are also unimpressed
with Russia's handling of the election.
All the terabytes of disinformation…
and every byte of it un-American…

Or maybe we are simply uncertain
we can go on living in this nation
that harbors people who believe
the members of the opposition

have sex with, and then eat, babies.
O I'm with you, brothers and sisters.
I too am discombobulated by it all…
disconcerted, feeling disenfranchised.

But… what if we also—despite being
disheartened—hold to an unwavering
love for home, the land of our birth,
dysfunctional as its governmental
systems and branches might be,

and so, we are yet unwilling
to give up hope of redoing
all of the terrible undoing
that has been done to it,

which brings me back
to the question buried
within our indecision:

Where and how would
we begin a new redoing?

Might I offer, unequivocally,
that we start by disselecting
the current Anti-Christ.

Turning Pale

~ for statisticians
Monday, October 19

Percentages change daily,
as if a million Americans
say to themselves, daily,
"Nope, I believe I'll vote
for that other one instead.
I find today's new Russian
algorithm too convincing."

The map of states moves
the reds and blues around.
Though, some swing now,
just like a Bob Wills song.

Texas turns to dusty rose,
with a dash of sunrise cyan.

Even that far northeastern tip
of our country's swollen thumb,
with its rocky Atlantic coastline,
is teetering on a sort of pink-ish.

My God, what next, Oklahoma?
I wouldn't cash in all my savings
bonds on that one anytime soon.

But what we will know, here
in less than three weeks, after
the two colors return to solid,
are the numbers of Americans
who would sacrifice—just like
those good much older days—
their children on altars to God;

and how many of us are left who
can still simply look a man square
in the bloody eyes, and caked on
blotchy face, and know exactly…
the kind of evil we're dealing with,
without the news having to tell us;

and not long after, we'll find out
how many have sworn an oath to
the most recent Aryan manifesto…
a creed of dipshit for dipshit's sake;

and then at some point beyond that,
we will begin to see what number
of our best and our brightest
are going to toss it in…
and make their break
for higher ground.

All in a Day's Voting

> Wednesday, October 21

It's more of an aversion,
a phobia, on my part,
than my brief poem
will have time for
deeply revealing.

But, nothing
will keep me
from doing my
constitutional deed
sometime tomorrow…
after Ashely wakes up…
because I'd not survive it
without her by my side.

First will be the *others*…
the people standing in line.
Then, those who'll scrutinize
my I.D. and squint at their list
to make sure I exist… within
the confines of their system.

And I'm preparing myself
for the ones who've brought
a careful, long-rehearsed stare

intended to politely intimidate…
because Darth Vader told them to.

There will also be the breathing
of their hot air to contend with,
and who knows where it's been.

But then comes the machine,
the box with a weird screen
that I'll not be able to read,
let alone comprehend, there
with its barrage of questions.

I am an inveterate monotasker.
It's why I hate games with timers,
split-screens and most conversations.

But, I will make my stand before it.
I'll have a picture of my daughter,
for the reminder of why I suffer.

I will go as slow as I have to.
Ash will finish ten minutes
before me. And yet, I will
find the correct button…
and push the damn thing.

The Full Armor

> Thursday, October 22

> Put on the full armor of God so that
> you can take your stand against the
> devil's schemes.
>
> ~ Ephesians 6:11

As I prepare to enter the gates
of the community center in town
and vote against the God of a good
number of my neighbors, and most
of the farmers and ranchers around
these here parts—a God of spanking
children and stoning unruly teenagers,
whose own son was blond, blue-eyed—

I've decided I should don the Belt of Truth,
for it has been in short supply in the weeks
and months of this insufferable campaign,

and also the Breastplate of Righteousness,
to protect me against the hollow points
they fire from pistols of ignorance…

both my feet fitted with readiness
and the Boots of Longstanding.

In addition, I shall take up the Shield
of Faith… to extinguish all the flaming
profanities hurled from the Trump booth.

And I will need the Helmet of Salvation
to protect me from their Covid breath,
as well as the Sword of the Spirit…
with which I will push that button,
in the hope of slaying their exalted
orange demon and all the slithering
sycophants writhing in his trousers.

> For our struggle is not against flesh
> and blood, but against the rulers,
> against the authorities, against the
> powers of this dark world…
>
> ~ Ephesians 6:12

I Voted

Friday, October 23

My access code was 27037.
The time? 1:30 PM—there
at, let's see, Precinct 337-B.

I needed to think like this,
in microscopic terms, one
number or letter at a time.

The initial screen indicated
that there would be 30 pages
to navigate with my little stylus.

The very reason I had to leave
the university—never to take,
nor teach, a class, ever again.

And, it was the first question
on the test, that felt like being
one of those two guys in charge

of the doomsday keys that unlock
the nuclear silo? and the other guy
has just been shot by the Russians?

and, now, you're standing there, frozen
in their sights? you know what I mean?
So needless to say… I paused over it.

I read those two names, trying so
hard to ignore the Independent
and Green candidates—who I

likely agree with on many issues,
but can't believe they were stupid
enough to muck with *this* election.

Probably 20 times… I read them…
my stylus quivering over the screen,
as if one wrong move could destroy

the world—a situation made worse
by being true. But I finally went in
for the kill. And I think my aim

was true. And I answered
the other 29, believing
that they matter too.

And I left feeling
empowered—even
with a sense my vote

has the chance of being
counted among watchdogs,
those with flags jammed into

every orifice of big-ass pickups.
And I left knowing this as well…
that whichever candidate wins it…

the fight will still be ours to fight…
the change, the hope of generations,
the difference… will continue to be

yours…   and mine…   to make.

GENERALLY SPEAKING

~ for Attorney General William Barr
Saturday, October 24

The generals
in the United States'
military would like it made
crystal clear (underline crystal)
that the second word in your title
is intended as a postpositive adjective
and not a rank, as it is in the armed forces.

Meaning, you're "generally" an attorney.
A point quite helpful to keep in mind
as we all consider what we think
about attorneys in general—

   apologies to the better
   ones among us—

and, as we all remember,
and consider, I'd like to make
sure you remember that honorable
is a quality earned, not appropriated.

Some may put it before your title
until they are red in their faces,
but it will never make it true.

As it is that I would also
like to brush you up on some
of the Latin you may or may not
have studied at Columbia, or George
Washington U. Do they for force you to?

    Qui Pro Domina Justitia Sequitur

flies on a banner beneath the wings
of an eagle on your big blue flag:

    Who prosecutes on behalf
      of the Lady Justice…

Do you remember? The one
with the scales and blindfold?

She, my dear little Willy,
is the one you serve.

Representation

~ for Nicole Lurea Cortichiato, and
U.S. Representative Alexandria Ocasio-Cortez
Sunday, October 25

So, I believe in gumption
forged out of impossibility,
how just the right amount,
and brand, of insanity...
and I imply, a beautiful
crazy... can vanquish
the pale and pudge that
infects political smugness.

And I believe in a woman
groping to find her way,
and policies, more than
I do a man who found
his so long ago? he can
no longer put a greased
palm on any one of them
buried in the slew of alibis
that pollute his sagging desk.

So when I pause to look over
the tops of my reading glasses,
much smaller than those huge

round ones she's made popular,
and I imagine what could secure
a place for my daughter, here in
the country of her birth, I think,

more bartenders named Sandy
serving as her representatives
in the United States Congress.

                That might do it.

Reclamation

> ~ for my friends in Oklahoma
> Tuesday, October 27

And then, there is
the death of trees…
which I refuse to see
as any less of a loss.

The ice gods arrive,
just as furious with us
as all the others, pillaging
through the night too early,
before the leaves have made
their pilgrimage to the ground,

and so… shattering decades of
my mother's dreams of green
and growing things just out
the windows of home…
the only theater screen
that thrills her anymore.

The red maple's limbs,
snapped and glorious
on the ground, all that
crimson and burgundy
ablaze behind the pane.

The ponderosa pine trees
she brought as saplings
from eastern Texas in
cut-open milk cartons
to always have a touch
of Longview near her.

And so they go, one
by one, as the earth
begins to take back
the billions of gifts
she so freely gave.

Reformation

> ~ for Darra Eek, and Konrad too
> Wednesday, October 28

After over half a century,
the weight of the world
came, all at once, to rest
on its broadleaf shoulders.

Not even the roots beneath
the house could anchor it…
not when comets made of ice
have sworn an oath to gravity.

And so the lean, then the crack
of earth, meets with the force
between two masses, which
are some distance apart…

and it comes in, limbs piercing
the roof, punching through walls,
not to kill, though it could have,
for one last gargantuan hug.

Goodbyes can be hell…
some of them more so
than others, but seldom
good, as the word hints.

My daddy planted that tree…
you told me, your voice barely
able to make it through those
seven excruciating syllables,

and now 2020 adds the realm
of absurdity to a never-ending
barrage of senseless cruelties,
as you pack up for a hotel.

But come spring, my friend…
if 2021 happens to pull one off…
there will be buds, even if they pop
and blossom in unfamiliar places.

And there will be green, even if
it covers much smaller limbs…
because the trees never give up.
Which, in the absence of better,

I guess, is a good lead to follow.

Mother of Exiles

> ~ for The Newer Colossus
> Thursday, October 29

Give me your tired
nurses, broken down,
crying in broom closets,

doctors who can't touch
their kids after working
so many hours, no one
really counts anymore,

and first responders
living on power bars,
coconut water and tea,

your poor nonessential
workers staring at that
last can of pinto beans
on a lower pantry shelf,

your huddled masses of all
those living with a number
of preexisting conditions,
yearning to breathe free,

even the wretched refuse
of those who refuse to see
the light of science and just
cover their damn mouths
or snot-dripping noses.

Send these... the ones
made homeless by Covid,
congress, a chief executive
self-proclaimed prick, floods,
hurricanes, wildfires, and ice...

the tempest-tost... to me.

I lift my lamp beside
the golden door!

A Fraternal Order of Sorts

> ~ for Brian Oakley, from Rain Flatt
> Friday, October 30

So, any son of a
southern preacher,
I hold as a comrade,
quite cautiously. Still,
you did escape it early,
even if by a kidnapping.

What I respect even more
is remaining a few hours shy
of a degree in English. Though,
the one you finished in economy
wasn't worth the wad you worked
your ass off to graduate with, I bet.

Ah university, the Costco of education.
Anyway, I'll growl "Go Sooners" if you
snicker "Hook 'em Horns." And then,
I will flunk one more football player,
while you don scrubs and head off
to do a thing that actually helps.

I have a PhD and still don't know
what a semicolon is for. So I'll not
start using them around someone who

is, I have heard, as particular as you are.
Hell, I'm not even sure I spelled it right.
I became a poet to avoid all the proper
applications of punctuation, and such.

But no matter how well versed I am,
how does one write a poem for one
who's won the O' Henry Pun Off
so many damn times, they filmed
a documentary about him? Well,
about his special problem at least.

And how can I trust a man who
has never had a cavity and loves
the godforsaken heat of Texas,
let alone goes out in the middle
of its hot nights to hunt hogs?

You make up for it, though,
with your appreciation for
giraffes and primo tequila.

And yes, the Hall & Oates
thing seems a bit strange.
But we agree on Buffett
and the Coral Reefers.

And look, this can't go on.
I'd just wanted to say that
life is hard on those who
use over 10% of the brain.

It's why we turn a bit crusty
and sardonic and don't enjoy
the Louvre. It's just too much
for hypercritical minds to take.

What I do like is the kind of man
who stops to aid the broken down.
Also, I trust a man who understands
the truth is more important than fact,
even if he does, in both truth and fact,
have occasional run-ins with sea turtles.

But, what I respect more than all of it,
is the man who, through every hard-
edged thing in life, has held fast
to the bastion of gratitude.

Tandem

~ for Celia Jones
Saturday, October 31

Sometimes the only way
for two people to get
from here to there
is for one to be
in front of
the other.

Even newly
weds get on
that 747 one
at a time, suit
cases in hands,
on their blissful
way to Bermuda,
much like two sky
divers leap, to keep
from getting tangled.

Like the two horses
in single file, in front
of a cart, makes sense.
But never two behind.

And though I'm not too
comfortable with the idea
of two people riding on one
bicycle… I've witnessed those
couples who have made it work.

So… if love were a canoe, which
I know sounds strange, it is better
to take turns, one in front paddling,
the second in back steering. Other
wise, we'd soon be treading water.

November ... ...

Every absurdity has a champion to defend it.

~ Oliver Goldsmith

Contingency

> Sunday, November 1

Where Texas reaches out
to the west, the arm it slid
under half of New Mexico,
the fat elbow pokes down in
to Chihuahua and Coahuila...
states just across a grand river,
on the other side of a treaty that
the United States never honored,
because they never did intend to.
Not as far south as, say, Laredo
or Key West. But, to my friends
up in Minnesota? well, I'll just say,
somewhere around South America.

We've come to the dust and rocks
of Terlingua—the end of that fat
elbow's universe—for what we
will call vacation if Joe Biden wins,
on Tuesday... or... to look for land
should Donald Trump remain king.
In other words, if the moon is still
unavailable for settlement, we will
want to head as far out of radar-
range as is physically possible.

THE BIGGEST BEND EVER

                    Monday, November 2

Dearest Don,

I feel the need to bring
to your short attention span,
on the night before the election,
that when it comes to your border-
line wall disorder, deep down in
the Big Bend of Texas, Mexico
has beat you to your sad little
punch.
        It's been working on
its security from us for some
100 million years. And, well,
I am afraid I must inform you,
it makes your delusional project
look like dental floss.
                      The cliffs
across the river there, in places,
rise to 1,500 feet, sheer stone
faces that could destroy us
in a staring contest.
                  I mean,
huge. Massive, more like it…

I'd say some of the hugest
cliffs you have ever seen…
possibly among the greatest
cliffs in the whole world…
beautiful… gorgeous cliffs.

So beautiful, you just wanna
swim over there and give 'em
a great big ol' kiss. You know,
if you're into that sort of thing.

Better Eons

                    Tuesday, November 3

So the Christmas Mountains,
across from Terlingua's better
known attraction, the cemetery,
look like God's old, abandoned
geological workshop, where he
first began experimenting with
the idea of hills and mountains.
Scraps mostly, of all the various
materials and mediums available
to him, back in the Precambrian,
or very late Stone Age, depending
on your religious predisposition—
strewn about and forgotten… after
he ran off to create the Swiss Alps.
And the Chisos Mountains below,
in the crook of a big bend in that
ocean receding into a river, look
to have been his first large-scale
endeavor, when he was still just
beginning to think about trees.
In other words, the very area
he will likely return to one day
when he grows dissatisfied and
disillusioned, and starts to get
nostalgic for the gool ol' eons.

THE LIGHTS OF MARFA

>Wednesday, November 4

I spent a chunk
of Election Day out
in Marfa, Texas, looking
for some kind of light. I cast
my vote days ago—like the line
on a fishing rod, not really believing
I'd catch anything worth keeping, but
hoping for better than Leviathan.

I walked around with Ashley
and a few New Yorkers...
not too hard to spot...
and happened upon
the lesser lights of
hazelnut-butter
fine chocolate,
and a vegetarian
street taco so good...
I knew this was no typical
tiny town in So Far West Texas,
the only thing below is Mexico
and the only thing above is
the newer version of it—
meaning very highly, yet
wonderfully, problematic.

We also found the strange
light of one well-supplied
liquor store that also sold
fresh produce, local eggs,
and organic gardening soil.

But Presidio County's known
for a lot of strange phenomena.

Among them? the odd, infamous
ghost lights that sometimes appear
just outside town, on Mitchell Flat.

But I will not catch those in daylight.
And besides, even they would not be
enough for what I am needing now.

CHISOS BASIN

Thursday, November 5

I spent the day after
the election in the now-
cooled basin of a volcano...
a symbolic, and fairly pleasant,
place to hike off those harbingers
of the news: that just about half of
the nation still wants an emotionally
crippled, playground-rich-kid asshole
to lead us through the valley of death.
A deep valley like I imagine this one
to have been, all those millions
and millions of years ago.
At the bottom of a long trail,
there's a huge window, between
colossal stone frames, that vented
the molten anger of these mountains,
in the days when they were protesting
a drastic change in the earth's politics.
A change much like the earth is soon
going to have to make once more.
Back to something... some age
before the final evolutionary
stage of a heating planet's
most regrettable species.

Roaming a Marathon

> Friday, November 6

Marathon sits on U.S. 90,
where it hugs the Southern
Pacific Railroad that rattles
the bones of just under 400
souls when it passes through
in the dark heart of the night.

The Gage Hotel takes up most
of the main drag. And though
this is no ghost town, Rooms
10 and 39, in the Main Hall,
seem determined to make
converts of nonbelievers.

Not the only game in town…
but the hotel owns the restaurant
next door, the bar next to that, and
the V6 Coffee Shop just beyond.

And though I'm not a believer
in any middle-of-nowhere…
it still seems strange to see
license plates from Florida
and California parked here
on the blacktop by the curb,

where the streets only run
as far north as 8th… and
as far east as Avenue J…

and where the one school
offers the older students
certification in welding
and pipe fitting, two
of possibly several
career paths for
a hundred miles
in every direction.

There is something
that remains, in towns
like this, of what America
could have never become—had
it not outgrown its founding britches.

Maybe that's why I love so much
to roam these eighteen streets,
then grab a latte at the V6,
and scribble about all
the things I miss.

THE LONGEST DAY

                      Saturday, November 7

Election "Day" is now
on its 105th hour… and still
no one knows which nightmare
scenario this country will inherit
next January.
            O, I tried to sound
more upbeat. But my pen is tired
of the orange poobah's grandeval
wailing and throttlebottom tweets.

The system is suspect, the process,
pernicious, the counters all crooked,
every one.
         And so, why can't he win?
Where did Russia go wrong… and…

where's that damn bucket of Kentucky
Fried Electoral Votes he ordered hours
ago?
    Dear God, just put him out of our
misery… and let us get back to the trials
and the terrors of a worldwide pandemic.

Too Much of 'It'

Sunday, November 8

It will be a couple of months
before I give some acceptance
speech.
      I need to see a hand on
a Bible, swearing to it—though…
I didn't trust it the last time I saw it.

The networks have now called it…
but I have never trusted them on it.

And while I do not believe this one
is the answer to all of it, I am quite
confident the last was the cause of
most of it.
      And because near half
of the country disagrees with me
on it? I know I'll spend the next
four years continuing to defend
my unusual angle on all of it.

Since there will never
be an end to it.

The Great Delay

~ for Sally Bass
Monday, November 9

It was out of the budget,
for a spring wedding in Texas.
But… when it's the winter before,
and we're looking for a little sunshine,
what're we supposed to do when we see
her face light up with it, and we feel it
radiate off of her, as she models that
dress—the one that is the one, and
not a thing can be done about it?

Then April comes, on the wings
of tiny airborne particles—forcing
everyone to shelter their excitement,
canceling all the best laid flight plans,
and steamrolling our rose-petal dream
for a big day of any sort… and, so…

vows are exchanged, somewhere up
in Chicago, with no family present,
and likely with a cold wind blowing
in over Lake Michigan, like it does.

And now the dress just hangs there
in the darkness of a mother's closet,

except for that little bit of light…

the light that bleeds in each time
she opens the door to put away
the day's shoes, and cry a little,

with tears she laces, at least,
with a quiet, glowing hope
for a day when the gods
allow us to gather again.

FEET IN THE FIRE

~ for Myra Spector
Tuesday, November 10

I have less time for fun
friends anymore. Friends
who might be anecdotally
entertaining, but take great
care not to ask any question
that could lead to some poet
formulating a kind of answer.
I've overlistened to far too many
champagne conversations and rosé
jokes by now. I'm ready for the burn
of my tequila's well-aged truth-telling
and the charred remains of a rummy
riddle that has no tangible solution.

I'd like to bring the stars down
around the fire and have them
tell us what we don't know yet,
but are damn well about to find
out, in this century, or the next,
about nuclear fusion and cosmic
radiation's dark sense of humor.
Just one of several reasons why
I have forged very few friends
in the smithy of my iron soul.

WHO'S WHO

> ~ for Myra Spector
> Wednesday, November 11

So, the Greeks have seven words
for love. They're better at ancient
myths and epic war poems too…
they've had a lot more practice.
That's why I hate the feeble way
my social platform of choice—at
the moment—only allows me to
have "Friends." And I may either
Follow or Unfollow them—things
I had never considered doing, back
in my previous and easier-going life.

Or, I can simply Unfriend altogether.
My God. The mind reels as I imagine
what I would have done with a button
like that, long ago… in the whatever-is-
the-opposite-of-halcyon days of 9th grade.

No, what I need more is something like
the Hundred Acre Wood of socializing.
Two buttons to differentiate between
all the Poohs and Piglets in my life.
You? I deem a Bear of Little Brain.
And you? You're one of the biggest

Worry Warts I have ever had worry,
incessantly, about, well, everything.

I'd have to have an Eeyore one too…
those who help me to feel understood,
as well as better about myself, because
I am, at least, not that far gone… yet.

And, if I had a mouse for every Owl
out there… the know-it-alls who don't
really know it all, but who think they do…
and so, are infuriating to those of us who…

But then, Lord have mercy, the Tiggers…
all that bounce and bad logic. These cats
would need a Hold at Bay button to click,
and I'd want a limit on the number allowed.

The Rabbits and Roos are important too,
but the most important selection of all
would be the Christopher Robin—
the very few, who are not always
around, but who make us feel
loved, and cause us to think
happy thoughts… even when
our heads're stuck in a honey jar.

Safe and Unsound

~ for Danna Primm
Thursday, November 12

All new windows
find you mostly inside,
but do an even better job
of keeping all others outside.

There's a stillness to the mandate
of caring for ourselves and others
these days that is, at times, almost
beautiful… so beautiful that we cry
most days, amidst bouts of out-loud
laughter, in the absence of any joke,
which concerns us somewhat. But,
there is no one who has to know.

And so you're on your 8th or 9th
time around the bases of all six
seasons of Downtown Abbey
while you chart the number
of daily cases, and deaths,
in Oklahoma, and 'Marie
Kondo' your shorts drawer
in the hall… where last week
you opened it to a live opossum.
The surprise was mutual, I'm sure.

We all need our quarantine stories,
and you damn well have yours now.

And though there was that daydream…
when you found yourself on stage jammin'
on a jimbe with Jahruba at a BLM rally,
(and, yes… it did actually happen…
you, gettin' down with your white
self…) you're still relatively wary
of the confusions and illusions
wandering the streets of late.

And a newborn abandoned
kitten you gave seven days
and a bottle to, kept things
real enough for an empath,
when, after all that, it died.

So, here we are. And where
is that, exactly? in this season
of reconsidering so many claims
we thought we'd meant at the time,

not the least of which would be:
"Don't call me… I'll call you."

WHEN SHE PRAYS

>Friday, November 13

In the chill of a November sunrise,
in the heart of the country's heart,
this poem will have to serve as
my prayer for one of those
days we spend our lives
trying hard to avoid.

Before dawn's light,
mom and I dropped
dad off at the gaping
entrance to a hospital
he had to take on alone,

because human ignorance
just loves to celebrate itself,
and so mom wasn't allowed
to go in with him.

>She wept
in the rear seat on the way
back to the house, where
the Brit in her did the only
thing there is to do at times
like this… put the kettle on.

We shared the first cup… then,
I came in here, to write a prayer
that may or may not go unheard.

And she retreated with a second
cup to her studio, where she will
offer up a prayer with better odds,

because she makes God more nervous.

When He Prays

>   Saturday, November 14

After bringing him home
from the surgery, I caught
myself trying to get between
him and the floor and the walls,
afraid he would hit, or bump, one
or the other, worried he might catch
the drain-tube sipping from the wound
behind his left ear on a cabinet knob
or the oven door.

>   He kept saying
he was fine, which more and
more, seemed to be true.

And when my dad prays,
in a soft cloud of comfort,
it is to a God that he's come
to accept is there after a lifetime
of study and conflicting arguments.

What a strange and miraculous thing,
when life gives a 55-year-old son
an 87-year-old father, who has
calmed the tempest waters
of a thousand Galilees,

and now calms
this wild new one
brewing inside me.

May I be so steady,
if I am able to row
the boat that far
to the other side.

When I Pray

> Sunday, November 15

it's with a pen, like this morning
out on the sun porch, while dad
read a crisp copy of the Sunday
paper with a flashlight, because
heavy winds and limbs knocked
the transformer out last night—
just 24 and some odd hours after
we wheeled him out of the hospital.

So the home-care instructions, for us
to read and carry out before bedtime,
required the same flashlight: empty,
squeeze, apply antibiotic ointment,
and get him comfy on his right side.
Things we won't need instructions for
by the time they're no longer necessary.

And so, when I pray, it's to the God
of candles and Covid, better times
and dying batteries—the God of
arbitrary disbursement of blessings,
who's always overwhelmed on Sunday.

Meaning that... when I pray...
I'm mostly talking to myself.

Dot Gov

~ for Oklahoma Governor Kevin Stitt
Monday, November 16

You often appear bewildered
by your election… as if saying,
"I didn't think it would be such
a big deal." Like a Beta Theta Pi
boy talking to police after a prank
turns deadly, the fraternity known
as a "rape factory" at Wesleyan U.

And, judging by your take on better
science, it seems you only sold those
"educational products" door to door,
and never once looked at a page of it.

Too harsh? Maybe not harsh enough?

Well, I'm simply taking my opportunity
—as a former gubernatorial appointee—
to slap you with the silk glove of poetry.

But know that it's personal as well—
you graduated from my high school
seven years after me, and I had this
gorgeous girlfriend who, religiously,
attended your father's church, down

by the river, where a terrible theology
tore our potentially good thing apart.

And I can't tell if you're dumb, or
stupid. The first seems to be less
intentional, like it's not your fault.

And yet spinelessness is quantifiable.

So, as Covid swallows your jurisdiction,
just know that, if it comes for my parents,
this poet plans to set your title straight…

        executioner.

Rudy, the Red-Faced

> ~ for Rudy Giuliani
> Tuesday, November 17

Your own daughter
describes the two of you
as being 'multiverses apart.'
I'm sure it could be her fault…
but, kids are a powerful testament.

In your brief career serving in the legion
of attorneys who are watching over
a President who mainlines
corruption using dirty
needles in the dank
alleys of a West Wing,
your neck no longer turns,
from whiplash and double takes.

So your eyes and shoulders now
have to compensate. And you
can't bend down far enough
to wipe that Ukrainian shit
off those stilettos you sported
as a transvestite nightclub singer.

But, it's not often we have a chance
to witness, on live broadcasts, the son

of Italian immigrants dissolve, before our
bloodshot eyes, like that German officer
in *Raiders of the Lost Ark?* Or, maybe,
more like a highly profane version
of the burning Buddhist monk.

And yet, your slow motion
version is much more
painful to look at.

ON CULTS AND KOOL-AID

~ for Emily K. Blackshear
Wednesday, November 18

You will find only one
Jonestown in Guyana…

since it is the third smallest
country in South America and
most residents came from India,
or belong to tribes like Wai Wai,
Patamona, and Wapishana.

And Jonestown was
a "thing," an event,
more than a place…
a way for yet another
sociopathic brain-snap
to murder 908 desperate
disciples who had followed
their god with slick black hair
and Elvis shades from San Fran
to the steaming jungle, and a utopia
where Christ was a Pentecostal commie.

The massacre that gave English the phrase,
Drink the Kool-Aid, which still is not funny.

What I hope to show, instead of tell,
is simply this: The moment we determine
to receive all—every last bit—of our news,
truth, and gross misinformation from one
man—a man who stabbed a neighbor's
cat to death when he was a weird kid
back in Indiana, and found it hard
to make friends—history tells us
how the party is going to end.

AFTERMATH

~ for Terry Clark
Thursday, November 19

With too many leaves left on limbs
and too much sap running in the veins,
no fire burns like a conflagration of ice
raining cold flames on October plains.

And now the battlefield is covered
in splintered bodies and severed
members that the traumatized
survivors stack on the curb.

Survivors who jump up
at every sound, and cringe
over the drone of chainsaws,
as they finish off the wounded.

Soon after come the high winds
sweeping down, to pick off
any staggering stragglers
still hanging around.

And, one man's heart
gives up from the strain
of cleaning out the debris
and trying to clear a path…

while another's breaks open,
as he stands with a rake in hand,
staring off into nothing in particular,
worrying about the state of his country.

New Fall Fashion

~ for Chick Morgan
Friday, November 20

For eight years,
black was the new
blue in the halls of the
white house, till Netflix made
orange all the rage for seven seasons.
But not even sixteen Emmy nominations
could prepare us for the big bloviating
orange that would take over those
white halls in his $8,000 navy-
blue jumpsuit, with a mind
dark as a moonless night.

And now that we've had
our chance to see all fifty
manic shades of that mad
jack-o'-lantern, we feel it is
finally time for a new black…
something more stylish… say,
in a small to medium decency,
with a collar of compassion,
that maybe brings together
the color complements
of relative sanity?

Hell Hath No Fury

~ for Patrick Marshall
Saturday, November 21

A mediator will say,
divorces work best
when parties agree.

Let us sign this thing
and enjoy the distance,
the peace that it brings.

But, when a chip has a big
childhood on its shoulders…
made of wealth and disapproval,

or, when a thorn has a damaged
ego festering in its side, just know
there'll be trouble in the courtroom.

As a lifetime Republican, he'd hoped
for a presidential disappearing act…
that the devil might go down to, say,

Georgia, or Mar-a-Lago, or maybe
sulk back to his cave on 5th Avenue.
But he's no idiot. He sees the news,

and what's coming. He knows the type
of American who believes the tweets.
And so, he is preparing himself for

the biggest tantrum ever thrown
in the hallways of Hell—a fit
fit for a king the size of

a wounded
child.

Until It's Too Late

> ~ for Barbara Ford
> Sunday, November 22

It's too soon to treat
every drop of water
like a glistening dime
put into a piggy bank,
or to plant another tree
for every one cut down.

And it's too soon to save
the mountain gorilla, or
the black rhino, or the
leatherback sea turtle,
or the Arizona agave,
or the western prairie
fringed orchid, or…

It is certainly too soon
to shut down windowless
conveyor-belt snuff-factories
where they mix sawdust and lint
into our children's chicken nuggets,
or to lean into the wind and the sun
to power our toaster ovens, when
dead and putrefying dinosaurs
still continue to do the trick.

It's too soon to link arms
in an unbroken "X" from
New York to Los Angeles,
and Seattle down to Miami,
and let the racist haters know,
this will be a hard cross to burn.

And, of course it is too soon to
look our grandchildren in their
eyes and say, Welp... sorry kids.
If they're still willing to talk to us.

Vast

> ~ for Jules Nyquist
> Monday, November 23

I-40, out west of Amarillo,
is a days-long remembrance,
a mighty vision of the Earth
without us… where it plans
to head back someday, too.

It is a half-continent made
of conjoined unfillable spaces
that not even Albuquerque, or
Flagstaff, can put a real dent in.

And the tumbleweeds will tell you
there's not much to hinder a man
from wandering off into oblivion.

I can't explain the fire that flashes
up in me when I blaze across that
1,000-mile testament to prehistory
so wild and stoic at the same time.

But, it has something to do with
why great horses have always
preferred it, to the barn.

The loss of these vast
open territories would be
the end of the better world.

But, as long as they hold fast
and hard onto their reigns…

I have at least one thing
to bring to the table
at Thanksgiving.

The Orangest

> ~ for Jan Ohmstede
> Tuesday, November 24

Let us bow our heads now
and give thanks this week
for the incessant beeping
noise of the bigly yellow
crane as it is backing up
and away from that Oval
Office in the White House,

finally extracting the most
orange, ever, fussy pants
from his cradle-rattling
hissy-rages, arms thrown
around the legs of his desk.

Let us celebrate that baby-blue
silence emanating from the seven
times he has gone golfing, while
the country smolders-in-place.

And let us say our grace
over the boys from Orkin,
with their red-diamond logo,
who will soon move in to begin
removal of the vampires and rats

still hanging above the rotunda
and gnawing holes in the wings.

And then, may we fan the smoke
from a green bundle of sage the size
of a school bus into every nook, crook,
and moldy cranny to ward off the dark
energy and Covid cooties… releasing
the bad juju to return to its master.

Wet Ingredients

> ~ for Karen Zundel, and Emma Gori
> Wednesday, November 25

Why does a batch of something
sound so wonderful? And why
does a handwritten recipe card
make the thing even more so?

But, if that recipe was written
by the hand of an Italian nonna,
who died more than 20 years ago,
the mouth begins to water without
even knowing what it's a batch of.
Some somethings are just a given.

And while dry ingredients never
amount to much on their own,
when you add eggs, and melted
butter, with the golden memories
of a grandmother's soft-baked love,
your gratitude knows no boundaries…
not even the one between life and death.

So, it's a batch of wafer-thin pizzelles.
And, how could anything be better
than something that is somehow
a waffle and a cookie at once?

LET US PRAY

> ~ for Thanksgiving Day
> Thursday, November 26

This morning I'm grateful
for this fried egg and faux
sausage I'm eating, slowly,
as I write with hot coffee.

But, I am deeply grateful
that I could afford them.

So, this poem should be
more a prayer for those
who cannot—for those
who will sit in their cars
in hours-long lines, eyes
peeled for any movement
up ahead, windshield wipers
pulsing in a flood of anxieties
over what might not be available.

And now… I feel the need to pray
for the ones in masks and ponchos
who are putting the boxes and bags
into their empty trunks and smiling
at a row of frowns in the backseat,
knowing… it will not be enough.

So… that has me wanting to pray
for those who will gather 'round
their big gold-dusted free-range
turkeys, sweet potatoes topped
with charred marshmallows and
candied pecans, Napa Valley rosé,
and slices of New York Cheesecake
from Ferrara Bakery, in Little Italy,

and who might believe that those
who are doing without this year,
are doing without by some fault
of their own lack of gumption
and hard work… because…

   we all need prayer,
  though we need it
for different reasons.

And now that you can see
how incapable I am of stopping
the tireless machinery of my mind,
I hope that you will pray for me…
and then give thanks with me…
for whatever it is we may be
fortunate enough to have.

BLACK FRIDAY

> Friday, November 27

This special day
I celebrate every year
by giving thanks for the many
things I no longer need to purchase
to assuage my frail self-esteem, or
to fill that incomplete space over
by the TV in the living room, or
to make my family and friends
feel guilty for not remembering
to get me anything for Christmas.
I go to no store for the holy season's
rock-bottom prices, nor to Amazon
for deals that, let's be honest folks,
will continue through to the next
Black Friday…   you know…
the one we hold in July now?

No, this day, for me, is about
coffee, the flat keys on a piano,
and moonless autumn nights,
crows, deep shadows, and
pen nibs wet with ink.

Besides, Black Monday
is just around the corner.

Better Than None

> ~ for Daniella DeLaRue
> Sunday, November 29

Sometimes, four days
can be enough. Especially
when it's four days more than
you had ever dreamed as possible.

They say good things come in threes.
Or is it twos? I suppose it depends
on who is counting? Whatever.
The thing is: you got extra.

Because of certain issues
a family in the Midwest will
never talk about… all you had
to go on was blue eyes, red hair,

vague references to Russian, Polish,
and because of a second DNA test,
Ashkenazi blood in your veins,
which led to a first cousin

that the test had revealed
was actually a half aunt, and
voilà… you have a grandfather
living in the suburbs of Chicago?

He's 97, when you meet, a year later.
And, for four days, you finally have
the chance to be a granddaughter,
the chance to find out that he had

been tying sailor knots all his days,
since serving in the South Pacific…
maybe in a subconscious hope that
one would hold until you got there.

So, you share ice cream, and pizza,
pictures, and stories… while sneaking
the best berries from the bowl together,
as you inch your chair closer and closer.

It was four days… one year ago now…
and he died this last August… one day
shy of a 98th birthday. In September,
you drove up to see his ashes off…

with full military honors. And then,
back at his house, an uncle pulled out
a jar from among a dozen or so bottles
on an upper shelf in his liquor cabinet.

Your grandfather had loved, and made
his own, brandied cherries… a secret

joy he'd spoon out two to three
at a time, in a long life of secrets.

And so, in your own stolen moment,
you pop the lid, and with a thin spoon,
partake of his loneliness, and his loves,
as well as all of a big family's secrets.

Just a couple were enough for you,
because you'd been given four days
and now understood the uselessness
of greed and its steady need for more.

A thing we all need to learn, as soon
as we can get around to learning it:

> There is a sweetness
> and satisfaction
> to… just
> enough.

In the Days of Our Redoing

> Monday, November 30

> Despair is, strangely, the last bastion
> of hope.
>
> ~ David Whyte

Our undoing
will be our demise
only if we remain undone,

and only if we continue to allow
that which did most of the undoing
to rage on in its campaign to undo us.

Though a tight squeeze, we have passed
through the sphincter of the election
of our discontent, intact, mostly.

And the result will not be
our redoing… it merely
buys us a pittance of time

to get to the redoing ourselves.
Resilience, at its core, is a revolt…
and revolts require citizens en masse.

Our children are asking us to lift them up
above the Dow Jones and the S&P 500,
and all our gross domestic products,

to offer them, simply, the chance
to have drinkable water, edible
food, and a tree in their yard

when they hit 60-something
and start stressing about how
their kids are going to survive.

For the current undoing will pale
in the blaze of the Great Undoing
if we do not set about, and rather

instantaneously, the big business
of cleaning up the damn messiness
we allowed ourselves to descend into.

And so, let us return, and revisit…
reacquaint, reassess… and then,
readdress that which undid us.

Let's reconnect, reinterpret,
with aim to reinvigorate,
what life is left to us.

Let the days of our despair
inspire a revolution of hope,
by the power of some volition,

that'll give us enough gumption
to get on with the one profession
we must devote these new days to.

These hours, and even minutes…
here, at the foot of our resilience…
in the necessary days of our redoing.

Also by Nathan Brown

In the Days of Our Seclusion: March – May 2020
In the Days of Our Unrest: June – July 2020
Just Another Honeymoon in France:
    A Vagabond at Large
100 Years
An Honest Day's Prayer
An Honest Day's Ode
An Honest Day's Confession
I Shouldn't Say…
Arse Poetica
Apocalypse Soon
Don't Try (with Jon Dee Graham)
My Salvaged Heart:
    Story of a Cautious Courtship
To Sing Hallucinated:
    First Thoughts on Last Words
Oklahoma Poems, and Their Poets
Less Is More, More or Less
Karma Crisis: New and Selected Poems
Letters to the One-Armed Poet
My Sideways Heart
Two Tables Over
Not Exactly Job
Ashes over the Southwest
Suffer the Little Voices
Hobson's Choice

Author Bio

Nathan Brown is an author, songwriter, and award-winning poet living in Wimberley, Texas. He holds a PhD in English and Journalism from the University of Oklahoma and taught there for over twenty years. He also served as Poet Laureate for the State of Oklahoma in 2013 and 2014.

He's published over 20 books. Among them is *100 Years, To Sing Hallucinated: First Thoughts on Last Words,* and *Just Another Honeymoon in France: A Vagabond at Large,* a travel memoir that marks the first in a coming series.

His anthology *Oklahoma Poems, and Their Poets* was a finalist for the Oklahoma Book Award. *Karma Crisis: New and Selected Poems* was a finalist for the Paterson Poetry Prize. And his earlier book, *Two Tables Over,* won the 2009 Oklahoma Book Award.

For more, go to: **brownlines.com**

MEZCALITA PRESS

An independent publishing company
dedicated to bringing the printed poetry,
fiction, and non-fiction of musicians who
want to add to the power and reach
of their important voices.

www.ingramcontent.com/pod-product-compliance
Lightning Source LLC
Chambersburg PA
CBHW020931090426
42736CB00010B/1103